Life in the Time of

Rosa Parks
and the
Civil Rights Movement

Heinemann Library
Chicago, Illinois

Designed by Kimberly R. Miracle and Betsy Wernert.
Printed in the United States of America in Stevens Point, Wisconsin.

052013
007400CPS

Library of Congress Cataloging-in-Publication Data
DeGezelle, Terri, 1955-
  Rosa Parks and the Civil Rights Movement / Terri DeGezelle.
      p. cm. -- (Life in the time of)
  Includes bibliographical references and index.
  ISBN 978-1-4034-9671-3 (hc) -- ISBN 978-1-4034-9679-9 (pb)
  1. Parks, Rosa, 1913-2005--Juvenile literature. 2. African American women--Alabama--Montgomery--Biography--Juvenile literature. 3. African Americans--Alabama--Montgomery--Biography--Juvenile literature. 4. Civil rights workers--Alabama--Montgomery--Biography--Juvenile literature. 5. African Americans--Civil rights--Alabama--Montgomery--History--20th century--Juvenile literature. 6. Segregation in transportation--Alabama--Montgomery--History--20th century--Juvenile literature. 7. Montgomery (Ala.)--Race relations--Juvenile literature. 8. Montgomery (Ala.)--Biography--Juvenile literature. 9. African Americans--Civil rights--History--20th century--Juvenile literature. 10. Civil rights movements--United States--History--20th century--Juvenile literature. I. Title.
  F334.M753P3735 2007
  323.092--dc22
  [B]
                                    2006102470

Acknowledgments
The author and publishers are grateful to the following for permission to reproduce copyright material: **p. 4** Corbis/Bettmann, **p. 5** Corbis/Bettmann, **p. 6** The Bridgeman Art Library/Private Collection/Photo © Christie's Images, **p. 7** Corbis, **p. 8** Corbis/Bettmann, **p. 9** Getty Images/New York Times Co., **p. 10** Corbis/Frances Benjamin Johnston, **p. 11** Corbis/Bettmann, **p. 12** Corbis/Bettmann, **p. 13** Corbis/Bettmann, **p. 14** Corbis/Bettmann, **p. 15** Corbis/Bettmann, **p. 16** Corbis/Bettmann, **p. 17** Corbis/Bettmann, **p. 18** Corbis, **p. 19** Corbis/Bettmann, **p. 20** Corbis/Bettmann, **p. 21** EMPICS/AP, **p. 22** Corbis/Flip Schulke, **p. 23** Corbis/Bettmann, **p. 24** Corbis/Arnold Newman, **p. 25** Corbis/Bettmann, **p. 26** EMPICS/AP/Joe Marquette, **p. 27** Corbis/Ariel Skelley.

Cover photograph of Rosa Parks reproduced with the permission of the Library of Congress. Cover photograph of school segregation protest reproduced with permission of Corbis.

The author dedicates this book to her Grandchildren.

Every effort has been made to contact copyright holders of any material reproduced in this book. Any omissions will be rectified in subsequent printings if notice is given to the publisher.

Contents

Some words are shown in bold, **like this**. You can find out what they mean by looking in the glossary.

Meet Rosa Parks

Rosa Louise McCauley was born on February 4, 1913. She grew up on a farm in Tuskegee, Alabama. Rosa became a **seamstress** when she was older. She married Raymond Parks and lived in Montgomery, Alabama.

Rosa Parks was a brave woman.

Rosa Parks believed that all Americans should have the same rights. She worked very hard for the **civil rights movement**. The civil rights movement worked to get the same rights for black and white Americans.

Rosa Parks is called "the Mother of the Civil Rights Movement."

Civil Rights

Slaves did not have any rights at all.

A long time ago in the United States, black Americans were **slaves**. The life of a slave was very hard. Slaves were forced to work for other people without any pay for their work. After the **Civil War**, slaves were free.

Many black Americans did not have a lot of money.

By the 1960s, black Americans still were not allowed to do all the same things as white Americans. Black and white Americans could not do everyday things together. Black Americans did not have the same rights as white Americans.

Separate but Equal?

Many Americans believed that people were equal, but that they should be **segregated**. Being segregated meant people could not do everyday things together. Black and white Americans could not drink from the same water fountain or use the same bathrooms.

These two men are drinking from separate water fountains.

Black and white Americans had separate entrances to buildings.

Black and white Americans could not even sit in the same waiting room. Black Americans had to sit in a different waiting room at the doctor's office or at the bus station. Their waiting room was usually in the back of the building.

Separate Schools for Children

Even children did not have the same rights. White and black children could not go to the same school. Black children went to schools that were very crowded. The students did not have desks or enough books.

Schools for black children were not as nice as schools for white children.

On May 17, 1954, the **Supreme Court** ordered schools to be **desegregated**. Desegregated schools meant black and white students could go to school together. Some people did not want black and white students to go to school together.

Some people were angry when black students started going to school with white students.

The Bus Boycott

Black Americans had to sit in the back of the bus. Sometimes they had to stand.

For a long time, black Americans had to sit in the back of buses. White Americans got to sit in the front seats. On December 1, 1955, Rosa Parks refused to get up and give her seat to a white man. The police **arrested** her.

Black Americans were angry and **boycotted** riding buses. A bus boycott is when people stop riding buses. Buses were empty because black Americans stopped riding. On December 21, 1956, the law changed and black Americans could sit in the front seats.

Black Americans did not ride city buses for 381 days.

Leading the People

Black and white Americans knew there had to be changes to make life better for all Americans. Powerful leaders were needed. A young **pastor**, Martin Luther King, Jr., wanted changes to come about peacefully without fighting.

Martin Luther King Jr. helped lead black Americans to get equal rights.

John F. Kennedy was president from 1961 to 1963.

The president at this time was John F. Kennedy. He knew that the country must work together. New laws were needed for changes. Black Americans wanted more rights. Americans had to work together for **freedom** and **equal rights** for all people.

Some Don't Want Change

Some Americans did not want change. They liked things the way they were. Some people wanted white and black Americans to be **separate**. Sometimes the two groups got into fights.

Some white Americans did not want black Americans to have the same rights.

Some white Americans did not want to be friends with black Americans.

Some white Americans did not want to work with, play with, or live near black Americans. These people did not know what black Americans were really like. They did not like people who looked different from them.

A Sit-In

On February 1, 1960, four black students sat down at a "Whites Only" lunch counter in Greensboro, North Carolina. Black Americans could not eat at a counter for white Americans. The waitress would not serve them. The black students would not leave.

This waitress is refusing to serve food to these black students.

This was the start of a **sit-in**. Students took turns sitting at the lunch counter for six months. On July 25, 1960, the restaurant **desegregated** the lunch counter. Finally, black and white Americans could eat in the same restaurant.

When the sit-in ended, white and black Americans could eat together.

Freedom Riders

Freedom riders were black and white Americans working together.

On May 5, 1961, a group of freedom riders got on a bus. They sat in the front seats. The law said black Americans could sit anywhere on a bus, but police did not make people **obey** the law.

When the bus stopped, angry people set the bus on fire. The freedom riders were hurt and **arrested**. On November 1, 1961, a new law said black Americans could sit anywhere on buses traveling in the United States. Police finally made people obey the law.

It was dangerous to be a freedom rider.

Gathering in Washington, D.C.

On August 28, 1963, black leaders **organized** a gathering of people in Washington, D.C. The gathering was peaceful. More than 200,000 black and white Americans came. Rosa Parks was **introduced** to the people as a leader for black Americans.

Thousands of people attended the peaceful gathering in Washington.

Martin Luther King Jr. gave a famous speech called "I Have a Dream."

Martin Luther King, Jr. told the people he wanted black and white Americans to live together peacefully. King said he had a dream that one day all people would be treated the same. People listened and agreed. They clapped, cheered, and sang songs.

The Civil Rights Act

Lyndon B. Johnson was president from 1963 to 1969.

On June 19, 1963, President John F. Kennedy sent a civil rights law to **lawmakers**. A few months later, Kennedy was killed. Vice-President Lyndon B. Johnson became president. President Johnson worked to give black Americans more rights.

President Johnson signed the
Civil Rights Bill into law.

On July 2, 1964, the Civil Rights Bill became law. The law said all Americans should be treated the same and fairly. Finally, black and white Americans would be treated equally. Things were beginning to change.

Equal Rights for Americans

Rosa Parks was honored in many ways for her work in the **civil rights movement**. She received many medals and awards. She was a hero to many people. On October 24, 2005, Rosa Parks died at age 92.

Rosa Parks received the Presidential Medal of Freedom award from President William J. Clinton.

Rosa Parks started the civil rights movement when she would not give up her bus seat. She worked most of her life in the civil rights movement. The civil rights movement helped make sure all Americans would be treated the same.

Rosa Parks worked to make the world a better place for all people.

If You Grew Up Long Ago

If you grew up in the time of Rosa Parks…

- You may have read about John Glenn, the first U.S. astronaut to orbit the earth.

- You may have seen Jackie Robinson, the first black American to play in major league baseball, inducted into the Baseball Hall of Fame.

- Your favorite television shows may have been *The Flintstones*, *Alvin and the Chipmunks*, and *The Jetsons*.

- You may have watched *The Ed Sullivan Show* and seen The Beatles for the very first time.

Timeline

1913   Rosa Parks is born.

1954   The **Supreme Court** orders schools to be **desegregated**.

1955   Rosa Parks is **arrested** for refusing to give up her bus seat.

1960   Four black college students begin a **sit-in** at a lunch counter.

1961   Freedom riders ride buses.

          November 1: The law says black Americans can sit anywhere on buses.

1963   August 28: Thousands of people gather in Washington, D.C.

          November 22: President John F. Kennedy dies.

          November 22: Vice-President Lyndon B. Johnson becomes president.

1964   The Civil Rights Bill becomes law.

2005   Rosa Parks dies at the age of 92.

Find Out More

Books

Dubois, Muriel L. *Rosa Parks*. Mankato, MN: Capstone, 2003.

Lynch, Emma. *Martin Luther King Jr.* Chicago: Heinemann Library, 2005.

Mara, Wil. *Rosa Parks*. New York: Children's Press, 2003.

Welch, Catherine A. *Children of the Civil Rights Era*. Minneapolis, MN: Lerner, 2001.

Websites

Academy of Achievement – Rosa Parks Photo Gallery

http://www.achievement.org/autodoc/page/par0gal-1

Library of Congress Kids – The Bus Boycott

http://www.americaslibrary.gov/cgi-bin/page.cgi/aa/activists/king/bus_1

PBS Kids – School Desegregation

http://pbskids.org/wayback/civilrights/features_school.html

Glossary

arrest take someone to jail

boycott stop doing something to show that you don't agree with something, such as a law

civil rights movement time in the history of the United States when black Americans worked to get the same rights as white Americans

Civil War (1861–1865) war between the Northern and Southern states of the United States

desegregate allow people to be together

equal rights when everyone gets to do the same things

freedom right to do and say what you want

introduce present someone to another person so they can meet each other

lawmakers group of people who make laws for a country

obey listen to and follow a law or rule

organize plan and get ready for an event

pastor leader of a church

seamstress person who sews things, such as clothes

segregate keep apart

separate divide and keep apart

sit-in sit someplace you don't belong to show that you don't agree with something, such as a law

slave person who is owned by and forced to work for another person

Supreme Court most powerful court that decides laws in the United States

Index